# Online Traffic & Advertisements

# Online Traffic & Advertisements

# Table Of Contents

Foreword

Chapter 1:
*Traffic And Ads Basics*

Chapter 2:
*Using Social Media*

Chapter 3:
*Using Content*

Chapter 4:
*Using A Press Release*

Chapter 5:
*Buying Ads*

Chapter 6:
*Free Ads*

Chapter 7:
*How Your Business Suffers If You Don't Have Customers*

Wrapping Up

# Foreword

When it comes to starting an online business with keeping the start up cost minimal one of the ways to get some attention to the site is through traffic. This is basically a system where sites are viewed in the exchange process that ensures the individual's site is part of that viewing arrangement. Get all the info you need here.

# Online Ads & Web Traffic

# Chapter 1:
## *Traffic And Ads Basics*

# Synopsis

This form of drawing interest to a site is both effective to a certain extent and also quite in expensive as it usually does not require any significant sign up fees.

There are also sites that also pay for visits though the sum is also insignificantly small. There are also offers received through emails that encourage the individual to click on the link ads that this too helps to drive traffic to the site quite effectively as most would be enticed to view the offers featured.

## The Basics

Being an active online surfer also help to drive traffic to the individual's site as there are some traffic exchange sites that cater to and encourage this sort of viewing style.

This is one way of being able to have a good understanding of what is popular and what is not in the online business arena. For those who use ads to gain further visibility for their products the online marketing style is also a good platform for getting this.

Due to the almost unlimited possibilities and with the ability to reach the target audience anytime and anywhere that has internet connections of course, this usage of ads has proven its merits.

In various ways the internet advertising can be rather profitable as it is a faster and easier way to keep track of the progress of the business online with the use of the various supporting tools.

Options such as blogs where there is the platform to interact with possible prospects who have the potential of eventually becoming loyal customers is a very effective way to getting the necessary interest in the business, product or service being offered.

# Chapter 2:
## *Using Social Media*

# Synopsis

Social media is fast gaining phenomenal popularity for the current generation and in most cases it seems to be the only mode of communications for those immersed into the online world. Business and leisure activities are both mostly conducted online thus creating a wealth of resources available to be tapped into.

## Social Sites

There following are several reasons why the social media has been able to establish itself as a very formidable platform for various intentions of communications on the internet:

Besides the more obvious reasons of being able to create the visibility for the business, product or service the individual is offering there is also the effectiveness of being able to create a "buzz" around the said elements to get even more interest in the individual's site.

This form of "advertising" can help to create a very effective and instant way of establishing a brand and raising the awareness of its existence.

The social media platform also provides the means to monitor the competitors' current pursuits and undertakings and helps the individual to make the necessary adjustments to his or her own site to stay competitive too.

This is also better facilitated due to the fact that actual advertising is rather limited and the focus is more on the actual exchange of information, comments and opinions which is usually popularly done with tools such as Twitter, Youtube, Facebook and other such platforms.

The perception of being involved on a more personal level allows the social media the distinction from other contact styles that also have the same end intention of promoting and creating visibility for their business entities to be most times better received by the masses.

Thus by tapping into the social media platform there are infinite opportunities to ensure the endeavor chosen to have a better chance of success because of the visibility this tools creates.

# Chapter 3:
*Using Content*

# Synopsis

In order to be able to create the visibility needed to stand out in the online arena content design has to have all the elements that would create the interest to ensure the viewers stay long enough to feel impacted with what is being presented. Therefore having well designed content material is a very important element to concentrate on when trying to establish the relevancy of a site.

# Content

Researching for information and finding out what are the current interest of the general viewing population is one way of making an informed decision on how the create the content for the intended site's postings.

When this is clearly outlined, then the process of creating the content can be embarked upon. Efforts must be put into ensuring the information being outlined in the content is not only interesting but has some accuracy and truth to it.

Simply churning out information to make up the content without proper verification will only create negative feedback and eventually cause the viewing traffic to stop visiting the site.

This can have a detrimental effect to the site's existence and when this happens it is often very difficult to reestablish some form of interest in the site again.

When the site's content is well thought up and designed, it also helps to establish the individual and the business as a serious entity and a formidable force that has the capability of garnering the desired interest through directing traffic to the site.

The intention of having a healthy percentage of traffic directed to the site would be to ensure the possibility of earning revenue through the conversion of the viewer into a loyal customer. In almost all cases this is the end desired targeted.

Therefore with this well established site solely based on the content material the individual is able to getting the online business visibility enough to ensure comfortable revenue earnings.

# Chapter 4:

*Using A Press Release*

# Synopsis

For some this may be a rather new way of going about getting the business site to the attention of the viewing public. Exploring the possibilities that can be harnessed by the use of the press release tool the individual may be able to enjoy the results of the advertising platform it presents.

# Press

The following are some reasons the press release style should be considered for its innovative and far reaching possibilities:

Press releases helps to create the firm presence of the brand online because more often than not it is directly tagged to the integrity of the business endeavor, thus ensuring the legitimacy of the content.

This also adequately gets the attention of all who are privy to access the internet platform.

Substantially increasing the visibility of the business online is also another reason to use this press release tool. The benefits of publishing something online would in all probability include to lower cost issue as compared to the more conventional way of organizing a press release.

The basis of the success would be through the relevant and popular keywords being included into the content of the press release thus ensuring the intended traffic will be efficiently directed to the site of the launch.

With the keywords the intended target audience can be easily reached and eventually converted to loyal customers therefore ideally creating the revenue earning possibilities.

All this in turn will contribute to the better SEO rankings which in itself is another beneficial factor. Being well ranked will help to encourage even more traffic to the site thus enhancing the visibility factor which is the target of the whole press release exercise.

In some cases free traffic is better than paid ones and this can be sourced through the various press release directories where the campaign can be posted for free.

# Chapter 5:
## *Buying Ads*

# Synopsis

There are several different types of ads that can be purchased for the further expose of the intended site to the target audience. However in using this platform the individual should be aware of the different styles and its benefits or not so beneficial features.

# Ads

Ads have always been and will always be an effective was to disseminate information to the masses at any given time. However one should be careful in how to handle the advertising campaign to ensure the ads don't become a nuisance instead of an advantage to the viewing audience.

Often visitors to the site are bombarded with unnecessary ads which instead of creating the curiosity in the individual viewer, it acts to turn the viewer from the ad being featured, thus effectively making the ad campaign a failure.

Buying one way ad links that are less intrusive may be a better alternative and it is less likely to cause the viewer to be irritated and thus turned off.

The main idea behind the ad is to effectively and quickly get the information across to the viewer within the small window of time usually allotted by the viewers concentration span.

Making the ads clear and concise, yet attention grabbing with all the right information clearly depicted, will enable the viewer to make the quick judgment to venture further into the site.

Including videos, graphics that are not too overwhelming, animations are actually quite a welcomed feature for most viewing participants as the often find this medium to be quite refreshing and engaging.

However these can be quite costly an addition therefore it needs to be carefully considered and designed well. This is to ensure optimization that will justify the high costs for using this particular tool to heighten the visibility of the endeavor featured.

# Chapter 6:
## *Free Ads*

# Synopsis

The obvious reason to use this platform is as it depicts, it's free. However just because something is free does not mean it is good, but this is the exception as free ads does have its own individual unique merits.

# Free Stuff

The following are some points to consider that highlights the merits of using free ads:

It's free – when there are no charges involved and no strings attached, there is nothing more attractive than being able to tap into this area to create a presence for the product, service or business online.

The cost saved through using this form of advertising can then be put into something else that would contribute positively to the overall business entity.

Using the classified links with the relevant information for the viewer to click on in order to understand and view more things that are being offered is also something that should be included.

This will satisfy the ultimate goal of drawing traffic to the site and also creating the possibility of encouraging the viewers to eventually become loyal customers.

The time saving element is also another plus point in using these free ads. It requires none of the more conventional methods of posting information and can be done online for a fraction of the time and effort when comparisons are made to other forms of listings.

Being easy to join and submit, is a feature that is important when it comes to enticing potential user to opt for this method.

This platform also provides for the ideal scenario to reach markets that would otherwise have not been possible to reach. The huge global market that can be assured of the viewing experience, simply due to the availability of such an attractive tool, is phenomenal.

However one should always consider the quality of the posting which should be neglected just because it is free.

# Chapter 7:

*How Your Business Suffers If You Don't Have Customers*

# Synopsis

Obvious or not, this statement is nothing to put aside, as it is a known and accepted fact that all businesses require the participation of customers on some level or another, in order to ensure its success.

Therefore the aspiring new business owner should take this matter into serious consideration and do all that it takes to keep the customer base interested and happy.

# Final Tips

There are several internet marketing tools available that specifically address the need to garner and keep customers. These tools should be carefully examined and chosen for its merits and contributing elements.

The tools chosen should also be fitting to the particular business endeavor it is meant to serve. In order to ensure the proposed business endeavor will be well received it would also be in the best interest to the potential business owner to do some research of the acceptance ration of the buying public against the product being touted.

Launching an item that is not going to be well received would be the same as heading into a business and failing even before it takes off. Therefore it is important to ensure whatever is being "sold" through the online business is going to be greeted with a ready base of preexisting customers.

Once this has been firmly established, the next step would be to consider the means of getting to these customers without having to incur costs that would be too high to bear for the startup online business.

Understanding the customers' needs and wants at the time would help to ensure that they are being adequately addressed through the purchase of the items within the online business endeavor, thus effectively and completely assuring the business of a set group of customers.

# Wrapping Up

Obvious or not, this statement is nothing to put aside, as it is a known and accepted fact that all businesses require the participation of customers on some level or another, in order to ensure its success. Therefore the aspiring new business owner should take this matter into serious consideration and do all that it takes to keep the customer base interested and happy.

www.ingramcontent.com/pod-product-compliance
Lightning Source LLC
LaVergne TN
LVHW021051100526
838202LV00082B/5456